Distance Learning:
Is it Right for You?

How it has changed and what you can expect.

by

Patricia Pedraza-Nafziger

Geek Girl Publishing

For more information contact **www.GeekGirlPublishing.com**

Cover design by Debi Gardiner of Gardiner Design

Distance Learning: Is it Right for You?
How it has changed and what you can expect.

Paperback ISBN: 978-0-9899042-0-9
eBook ISBN: 978-0-9899042-1-6

Published in the United States of America

ACKNOWLEDGEMENT

To BellaOnline – The Voice of Women

Thank you for providing an environment for women to share
knowledge on topics they are passionate about.
I am very pleased to be a part of the BellaOnline family.

"Every Accomplishment
Begins with the Decision to Try."

--Anonymous

INTRODUCTION

During the past decade there has been a substantial increase in the number of students participating in distance learning (DL), also known as online learning (OL), programs offered by universities globally. The popularity of learning in this type of environment can be attributed to the fast-paced evolution of information technology and social media which shows no sign of slowing down anytime soon. With the variety of communication and collaboration avenues available to educational institutions, universities are better equipped with the necessary tools required for instructors and students to better connect with one another in a virtual setting.

A number of virtual communication tools are available to enhance online learning and create a learning environment similar to attending a classroom setting; these include viewing prerecorded lectures, attending virtual classrooms with the use of avatars, using chat rooms, posting on discussion boards, and watching live video communications. This type of learning environment can broaden students' perspective by having them collaborate in a venue comprising individuals who are located worldwide.

Before potential students consider participating in a distance learning program, it is essential for them to have a basic foundation of computer skills such as sending and receiving emails and creating text documents/presentations, as well as some experience in searching the web for data which will be used for research purposes because assignments typically require references to be provided. If a classroom student considers making the transition to a DL student, he or she must also understand the importance of time management. A typical DL class will require students to fulfill weekly discussion assignments, provide feedback on a minimum of assignments provided by their virtual classmates and complete a weekly written assignment. This is all in addition to the online research or readings that will also be due each week. Maintaining this pace can be challenging, particularly if a student is attending a program full-time and required to juggle a number of classes.

Despite these requirements, the convenience of choosing a distance learning program can be of great benefit for busy individuals: students who also have full-time jobs, full-time mothers, and those simply wishing to reside near their families while attending college. Due to the increased demands in people's lives, many top universities are beginning to deviate from their traditional teaching methodologies and are starting to embrace distance learning and online education by offering certificate programs, degree programs, and advanced degree options online. Many universities will also require the students to attend several residencies each year where students meet at a university or venue of choice for workshops. This time should be used as an opportunity for students in the same discipline to collaborate face-to-face.

Compared to traditional brick-and-mortar teaching institutions, distance and online education is on the rise and is proving to be an effective method of education. Distance learning can be a rewarding experience equal to and perhaps even greater than education in a traditional classroom environment. *Distance Learning: Is It Right for You?* will provide the basic knowledge you need to ease into your distance learning experience. Topics discussed include types of distance learning delivery methods, financial aid resources, degree options available, necessary tools for distance learning, skills used and acquired in distance learning, the importance of health and education, and a list of top universities offering free distance learning courses so that you can get a taste of how you might adapt to a distance learning environment. Before making your decision, review this book and consider your own strengths and weaknesses to determine whether distance learning is the right choice for you.

PATRICIA PEDRAZA-NAFZIGER

DISTANCE LEARNING

Top Misconceptions About
Distance Learning

Though the popularity of distance learning has increased dramatically in the past decade, there are still some misconceptions about it. These erroneous beliefs lead some potential students to rethink the distance learning path, while others enroll in distance learning courses because they feel that these classes are an easier option.

One common misconception that students and job recruiters have about distance learning is that the courses are easier than courses offered on campus. Sure, students gain time benefits by not commuting to and from school, but, in reality, distance learning courses can be more labor intensive. Students learning on site fulfill most of their class discussion requirements within the class timeframe. Distance learners are expected not only to post their viewpoints on the topic via discussion boards, but also to read and respond to their classmates' posts. Additionally, instructors expect writing to be in excellent grammatical form to receive full credit for discussion posts. Sounds easy compared to voicing an opinion or two in class? Think again.

Another common misconception is that employers will not accept a distance learning degree. Many distance learning programs are accredited. Accreditation is a process by which peer review organizations, such as the Accreditation Board for Engineering and Technology, Inc., evaluate educational institutions and specific programs. Many corporations fund tuition reimbursement programs for accredited institutions, including distance learning programs. If you take classes through an accredited program, the quality of your education is less likely to be questioned by job recruiters regardless of its campus.

Many potential students are under the impression that being technology savvy is necessary for participating in today's version of distance learning: e-learning. The fact is, many interactive e-learning modules available as distance learning courses are very user friendly. Most lectures include narration and simple navigation instructions for technology novices. Some universities still require textbooks, many are opting to use student e-books. The majority of your distance learning curve will relate to how well you operate your own personal computer or tablet. If you use the Internet regularly and occasionally send e-mails to friends or relatives, you're off to a good start.

Another misconception is that students who participate in distance learning programs are solitary learners who have no interaction with other classmates. Although parts of your distance learning program are solitary, such can also be the case with brick-and-mortar classes. When you complete an assignment, you are typically in a solitary environment or working alone. However, similar to onsite classes, distance learning courses require that you have chats or discussions with your classmates and sometimes even use video conferencing to participate in class discussions with your peers and your instructor. In distance learning, interaction with others is a large part of the program; it is simply a different type of interaction, one that parallels today's high-tech society.

The type of educational venue you decide on is really a personal choice. Busy individuals who want to advance their education find distance learning the way to go. Younger students who look forward to the college experience may be better suited to attend a traditional university. Whatever your decision, know that both avenues can provide you with a quality education.

Delivery Methods for
Distance Learning

The concept of "What is old is new again," seems to ring true, especially when it comes to processes involving the use of information technology. Historically, certain processes required the physical on-site presence of an individual to be completed. The following are just a few examples of how lives have been simplified because of the change in delivery method:

- Online Shopping in lieu of mail order catalogs

- Video streaming services in lieu of video rental stores

- Craigslist and eBay in lieu of newspaper or magazine classified ads

- Travel websites in lieu of travel agencies

- Wikipedia in lieu of an encyclopedia

- Search engines in lieu of library microfiche

- Text messages in lieu of telegrams

- News aggregators in lieu of newspapers

- Distance (online) learning in lieu of correspondence courses

Although it may seem relatively new, distance learning (DL) has been around for centuries. The delivery method for DL has changed from a dependency on postal services and satellite campuses to communicating with classmates in real time and worldwide through the touch of their fingertips.

It is not too surprising that the naming conventions vary depending on the means by which education is delivered, i.e., from classroom instruction to correspondence courses to distance (online) learning. There are a variety of labels used to describe DL processes today, including the following:

- **Synchronous Distance Learning** is real-time DL, whether in a classroom or virtual, through live communication.

- **Asynchronous Distance Learning** is learning performed at your own pace but guided by a designated schedule that ensures the course will be completed on time.

- **Broadcasting Courses** are courses that use television or radio as a means to broadcast lessons in correlation with face-to-face and independent learning.

- **Teleconferences** and **Videoconferences** are used in DL for collaborating with fellow students and making presentations and as a means to view live lectures.

- **Hybrid Distance Learning** (aka **blended learning**) is independent DL in which lessons and learning activities are performed online. Typically, no classroom instruction is required unless the degree program requires a student to attend an annual face-to-face residency of some sort.

- **e-Learning** is technology-supported learning (TSL) utilizing various forms of computer technology tools to provide communication and collaboration with classmates and instructors.

- **m-Learning** is technology-supported learning via mobile devices; it is a process similar to e-Learning.

Despite the delivery methods used and associated labels provided, they all fall under the family of distance (online) learning, and as technology continues to evolve, so will the list of methodologies available for an online DL education. The key to making your learning experience a positive one is to use the method of delivery that best suits your lifestyle.

FINANCIAL AID

PATRICIA PEDRAZA-NAFZIGER

Student Financial Aid

In the past several years, the economy has faced its fair share of struggle. Parents who set aside money for their children's college educations were faced with the possibility of losing their livelihoods, leaving the children to establish their own plans to pay for college. Many individuals in the workforce found themselves having to go back to school to learn a new trade, while others work several jobs to attend college part-time. Let's face it: college is expensive and, for the majority, necessary to sustain a long-term, prosperous career.

There are several ways for individuals to obtain money for college. These include college/university financial aid, corporately funded tuition, scholarships, and federal student aid. The U.S. Department of Education is the largest provider of grants, loans, and work-study funds for students. Every January, the financial aid application process begins. The process is straightforward. Go to **FAFSA.gov** and begin the free application.

The following choices for financial aid are available:

- **Student Loans:** While similar to regular loans, student loans can only be used for college or training and must be repaid in full with interest.

- **Grants:** These provide students with money that does not need to be repaid. However, qualifying for a grant is based on financial need.

- **Scholarships:** Given to students who excelled in high school, scholarships are cash awards that do not need to be repaid.

- **Work-Study:** These grants give students an opportunity to work a part-time job, sometimes in their fields of study, and allow students to earn money to help pay for their education.

There are a variety of loans, grants, and work study programs available, each with their own unique eligibility criteria. Although the primary qualification is that the individual has financial need, there are other prerequisites. A student must be a U.S. citizen; if an international student, he or she must have a Green Card or T-VISA. Additionally, a student must have a high school diploma or general equivalency degree, be enrolled in a university program, registered with selective service if male, have a valid Social Security number (with exceptions), and maintain passing grades while in college.

If a lack of funds is the only thing holding you back from pursing a college education, please visit the Federal Student Aid website at **http://studentaid.ed.gov/** to learn more.

Tuition Reimbursement Programs

Distance learning students comprise a variety of age groups from fresh out of high school to senior citizens. Many students who participate in distance learning choose it as a time-saving convenience, especially for those who are full-time employees seeking advanced degrees to assist in their career development. Many companies offer a tuition reimbursement program for a variety of distance learning degree and certificate programs.

The majority of companies will only fund employee education if it pertains to an area of study to be utilized within the company. In other words, the company feels it is investing in itself by offering this benefit to employees, but it is important to plan a career path that is best for you as well. Planning a long-term career path is the first step toward determining a degree program that may work best for you.

Schedule a meeting with your manager or career-development advisor to help you cultivate a five-year development plan. Doing this will not only help you resolve whether the area you plan on studying is the right fit for you, but it will also help you institute a better understanding of your personality, skills, and interests to ensure that your selection will be your best career option.

Once you've made your decision on a specific career direction, you can then settle on which degree program will help you achieve your goal. When you have narrowed your range, your next goal is deciding on a university that offers that program via distance learning. Corporations are beginning to embrace accredited universities that offer full-time distance learning degree options, so prior to selecting a school, ensure your institution of choice falls under the corporation's preferred schools list. If it does not, your tuition may not be covered, or you may require a higher-level manager's approval, which typically requires a justification letter.

Once you have your university and degree program selected, you're ready to apply and, we hope, be accepted into the program. Upon completing this process and are ready to register for classes, ensure you understand your company's policy on the annual tuition cap. If you register for too many classes in one year, you could be responsible for paying the excess tuition fees. Furthermore, in order to receive a tuition reimbursement for each class, you need to maintain a specific grade-point average. Typically, the average grade requirement increases per level of the degree program (i.e., C average for bachelor's degree, B average for master's degree, etc.). Check your company's policies and guidelines to determine restrictions or limitations to your company's tuition reimbursement program.

The Value of Accreditation

Accreditation is a process by which educational institutions or specific programs are evaluated by peer review process organizations such as Accreditation Board for Engineering and Technology, Inc. (ABET) or Higher Learning Commission (HLC). The accreditation process has been utilized for over a century. It was originally established to ensure the quality of education provided by secondary and postsecondary educational institutions. Choosing an accredited university means a quality education and greater career opportunities.

When undertaking the process of selecting a university, it is essential to consider the institution's accreditation status. The selection of an accredited university assures that credit hours and courses can be easily transferred to another university should one decide to pursue education beyond the bachelor's degree. Typically, credits from nonaccredited programs are not transferrable to accredited universities. Additionally, many federal student aid and student loan programs will only fund accredited programs, further necessitating the selection of an accredited university.

The importance of selecting an accredited institution is also true when choosing a distance learning degree option. The following universities are accredited and offer a variety of degree levels and program options:

- **Capella University** offers high-quality undergraduate, graduated, and certificate programs in the areas of business and technology, education, health care and nursing, counseling and psychology, and public service.

- **Kaplan University** has a wide variety of degree programs in the fields of arts and sciences, business, criminal justice, education, health sciences, legal studies, nursing, and technology.

- **DeVry University** provides degree programs on-site as well as online. Online programs consist of business and management, engineering and information sciences, health sciences, liberal arts and sciences, and media arts and technology.

- **Walden University** has degree levels ranging from certificates to doctorates. Degree programs consist of business and management, communication and news media, counseling and human services, criminal justice and emergency management, education, health sciences, information technology, nursing, psychology, and public policy and administration.

- **Ashford University** provides degree programs on-site as well as online. Online programs consist of business and professional studies, education, health and human services, and science and liberal arts.

DEGREE OPTIONS

Associates Degree

Today, there are many two-year degrees that provide students with the education needed to obtain a relatively high-paying job: registered nurse, respiratory therapist, computer programmer, police officer, paralegal, industrial engineer, technician, dental hygienist—the list goes on. One commonality among these two-year associate degrees is that they offer students the chance to continue on to a four-year degree should they so desire. An associate degree is a two-year undergraduate degree offered by community colleges, universities, and junior colleges, and is a degree students can earn on campus or via distance learning online. Although many younger, tech-savvy students fresh out of high school would enjoy the mobile lifestyle online courses afford them, the first two years of college are such a vital part of the socialization development process that there is really no substitute for attending classes in person.

During the first year of an associate degree program, students are offered a wide range of courses designed to expose them to writers, thinkers, arguments, debates, artworks, books, they might otherwise have not encountered. The usual reading and writing, mathematics, and sciences are all requirements, but classes such as art, music, philosophy, public speaking, nutrition, women and society, and oceanography, just to name a few, can be taken as electives. These courses offer students the chance to branch out into other areas and decide whether the degree programs they are pursuing are right for them. Especially for those who have just graduated from high school, attending the first year of college on campus can help them meet new friends and expand their social spheres. Campuses offer different experiences than other social networking environments offer. For baby boomers and Gen Xers who return to school for retraining purposes, or for mothers who have raised kids and are ready to try something new, pursuing an associate degree online is a great choice. However, everyone should try taking an evening course on campus just to experience learning in a multigenerational classroom.

Although many technical and business schools offer fast-track options that will allow students to graduate in one year rather than two, accreditation should always be verified. Students need to ensure the degrees they earn will allow them to continue their educations if they eventually apply to four-year colleges. In the meantime, deciding to pursue an associate degree is a great way to both begin an educational journey and qualify for a job that will pay a decent salary. As much as we all desire a comfortable livelihood, it is equally important for people to choose occupations they enjoy. Students who are unsure about which direction to go may consult with career counselors at local universities or job fairs. They can assist with decisions on the best degree options.

Bachelor's Degree

Many people who have completed their associate's degree will eventually decide to continue on with a bachelor's degree, whether for a change of career or to qualify for a promotion. There are many benefits for college students who have completed their bachelor's degrees such as higher earning potential, employer-provided health care coverage, job satisfaction, job stability, and less stress and lower blood pressure due to making healthier lifestyle choices. College graduates are also more competitive among their peers.

A bachelor's degree is a four-year undergraduate program. There are many bachelors' programs available on college campuses and even more options available through distance learning. The number of credits required is on average 120, or about forty courses. Most of the courses taken in a bachelor's program are general ones, including mathematics, science, language, and social sciences, while the remainder of the courses surround the discipline and major that the student has chosen. The most common bachelor's degrees are the Bachelor of Arts (BA) and the Bachelor of Science (BS). Bachelor of Arts degrees are awarded to students who major in the arts, including the humanities, music, and social sciences. The Bachelor of Science degree is awarded to students who have majored in the physical, mathematical, or computer sciences. Other bachelor's degrees are offered in specific subjects such as the Bachelor of Fine Arts, the Bachelor of Education, and the Bachelor of Engineering. Whether pursuing your bachelor's degree online or on campus, your typical learning objectives will be the same except for a few minor considerations.

During examination time, many local universities that offer bachelor's degrees online will require students to complete writing projects or exams on campus. These are often located in a special testing area monitored by a video camera and a microphone. It is standard practice to only allow a pencil, pen, and blank writing paper into the examination room. Other items, such as a handbags, cell phones, books, calculators, and backpacks, are left in a safe place with university personnel until the timed exam is complete. Before entering the examination room, you must first provide proof of identification, such as a driver's license, and sign a document that releases the examination to you. The testing administrator also signs the document and then writes down the testing start time. Depending on the type of bachelor's degree you are pursing, you may be required to spend different amounts of time on campus for requirements such as library research, labs, and group activities. Much of what you learn during your pursuit of a bachelor's degree will be useful in your future career and even in your personal life. You will acquire many skills, including problem solving and persistence, which will be necessary throughout your career. Most important, learning is fun and getting your bachelor's degree will start you on a path to lifelong education.

Advanced Degrees

After dedicating several years of hard work to pursing your bachelor's degree, you finally land a job in the field you've dreamed of entering. Having spent a number of weeks becoming acquainted with coworkers, you learn that many of them have earned not only bachelor's degrees, but also advanced degrees such as master's and doctorates. Discovering that you are surrounded by such a highly educated team, you realize that you're both the new kid and one of the least educated people in your office. Subsequently, when the two of you first meet to discuss your performance, your new boss enlightens you about the many benefits of obtaining an advanced degree, both for your career and financially.

Today, more individuals have attained advanced degrees than ever before. Due to this fact, becoming a competitive job candidate may require you to hold an advanced degree. If you are already employed by the company you most desire to work for, take some time to explore the career advancement opportunities your company provides, and the steps required to take advantage of them. There are normally a range of both management and nonmanagement positions that are challenging, prestigious, lucrative, and satisfying. Consequently, establishing a long-term plan is essential if you are to reach your goal. Many companies offer their employees a tuition reimbursement plan, allowing them to pursue advanced degrees on the company's dime.

Pursing an advanced degree can lead to many personal and professional benefits. Individuals with graduate degrees typically rake in thirty percent more per year than people with bachelor's degrees alone. Additionally, a graduate degree will command the respect of your peers and, more importantly, your higher-ups, who will regard it as a sign of your discipline, intellectual prowess, and ability and willingness to handle challenging environments. Your sense of accomplishment will set you on a path as a lifelong learner. After obtaining master's degrees, many people ask themselves, since they have already worked so hard, why not sprint toward the finish line and obtain a doctorate?

The decision to pursue a doctorate is an educational commitment like no other. Individuals who choose to continue onto a doctorate typically plan to become professors, researchers, and scholars. Many who wish to teach at the university level will require a PhD in order to do so. Researchers are critical thinkers who use their knowledge to mount arguments about particular research areas and publish their findings. Scholarship can involve producing new knowledge, writing or coauthoring textbooks, peer-reviewed articles, monographs, and conference presentations. Electing to pursue a doctorate essentially means committing to a life of learning.

If you are wondering whether to pursue an advanced degree, discuss your thoughts with your company career counselor. He or she should help you determine which discipline best suits your long-term goals. Pursuing an advanced degree is a serious, long-term commitment, so be patient with yourself, and understand that the time invested will contribute to your personal growth for years to come.

Choosing the Right Online Degree Program

Selecting a degree program can be a daunting task, particularly if your area of study covers a variety of disciplines. One way to help narrow down your choices is to visit a career counselor who can help you better understand your interests and long-term goals. Even if you feel like you have a basic idea about your academic plan, you may still be able to learn from discussing different degree options with a counselor. Finding a career that fits your interests and strengths, one that intrigues and challenges you, is not always an easy thing to do.

Let's say you've made the decision to get a degree in computing and technology because you are fascinated with computers and all they have to offer. You begin by browsing the web for universities that specialize in degrees in various areas of computing and technology. First and foremost, you should select a university that provides an accredited education. Attending an accredited university means that you are more likely to achieve a degree that recruiters and employers recognize as a quality education, thus improving your chances for better career opportunities. Search for the "25 best online computing schools," for instance, as a good starting point.

When you have narrowed the field down to a few of your top choices, it's time to review and compare the degree programs thoroughly. To follow our example, you should conduct a bit of research in the field of computing and technology to get a sense of the variety of disciplines offered. Here are a few degree options, including brief descriptions:

- **Computer Science (CS)** focuses on the design and development of computational systems, such as intelligence systems, robotics, and bioinformatics.

- **Information Systems (IS)** addresses the needs of businesses and enterprises by integrating technology solutions and new business practices to improve productivity.

- **Software Engineering (SE)** is the process of designing, developing, maintaining, and testing software, using the principles of engineering.

- **Computer Engineering (CE)** focuses on the design and development of hardware-software integration by utilizing both electrical engineering and computer science.

- **Information Technology (IT)** covers a broader scope of computer technology needs in the government sector, private sector, schools, health care, and other types of organizations.

Although the above disciplines are all part of the computing family, each one comes with a different area of expertise and a different set of expectations. In the fields of Computer Science, Computer Engineering, and Software Engineering, the most important courses required will be computing courses, such as programming languages, mathematics, and algorithms. On the other hand, Information Systems and Information Technology will emphasize several non-computing classes, such as Decision Theory, Organizational Behavior, Business Models, and Interpersonal Communication, in addition to the core computer courses. Knowing the course requirements for each discipline will help give you an idea of how complex each field is, which may help you narrow down your choice.

Prior to selecting your degree program, it is not a bad idea to do some research to ensure that your area of study is sustainable. Many areas of computing and technology are only short-lived trends, while other technologies are part of prolonged evolutionary processes. The idea is to ensure that the technologies you are studying will still be available when you achieve your degree. To improve your chances, try to diversify your areas of study to help broaden your scope of knowledge. For instance, add a minor in business to a major in computing. This will not only provide you with a broader foundation of knowledge, it will also help cast a wider net for future career opportunities.

Residencies and Colloquiums

Distance (online) learning affords convenience for the average student since it saves time by eliminating the need to physically attend class. Nevertheless, there are few distance learning programs available with a "no attendance required" policy. Most programs will call for students to attend the university or a designated meeting area at some point during the course. All universities establish their own requirements for physical attendance, ranging from once each week, once each quarter, once each semester, or once a year. These meetings, or seminars, are commonly referred to as student residencies or colloquiums.

Distance learning residencies are typically held at the university campus. Some universities may choose to conduct their residency at another location, such as a satellite campus, which offers convenient travel for its students. Depending on the type and area of study, residencies are sometimes even held internationally. Attending a residency offers students an opportunity to visit the campus to learn more about the school's history, interface with educators, and use the residency as a way of building relationships and networking. In the long run, this helps provide motivation and support for one another.

Colloquiums are similar to residencies; they are scheduled seminars that students and faculty participate in for networking, lectures, and workshops. Colloquiums are normally held at a hotel venue at which lodging, meals, and conference rooms are available under one roof. On the first day, an agenda is provided to each student along with a name tag and coursework/workshop materials. At times, even breakfast and lunch are provided in a large hotel dining room where students can mingle and interface with peers and faculty on a more personal level.

Attending a distance learning residency or colloquium can help students enhance their understanding of the coursework by communicating in a group environment with fellow students to share ideas, work toward common goals, and even develop a project together that may be presented on the last day. Since residencies and colloquiums are held within a limited timeframe, the coursework tends to be demanding, so be prepared for intense study sessions.

The time required to attend each residency or colloquium can range from a few days to a few weeks. Working professionals must plan their vacation schedule and budget ahead of time to ensure they are prepared to attend their required residency or colloquium. If the company you work for offers a tuition reimbursement program, there may also be an opportunity to attend on company time if the degree program enhances your current occupation. Take time to review your company's education and training policies to learn more.

MUST HAVE TOOLS FOR
DISTANCE LEARNING

Equipment and Applications (Apps)

So you have made the decision to pursue your degree online. Before you get started, there are a number of tools you should become familiar with to help you in your journey through distance learning. The goal is to become accustomed to these tools so you are better positioned to make the most of your educational experience without the distraction of dealing with the new-tool learning curve.

Mobile devices, such as laptops or tablets, are great tools if you tend to be on the go and find public places, such as local coffee houses, libraries, or restaurant lounges, comfortable places to study. However, if you are participating in online courses that require multiple hours behind your laptop, you will be better suited ergonomically using a flat screen monitor, so try saving your lengthy projects to work on at home. This will help you reduce the effects of computer vision syndrome and other ergonomic issues that can arise after repetitive lengthy study sessions.

Throughout your distance learning program, you may participate in some courses that require student interaction via videoconferencing, such as Skype or WebEx. Most universities use communication software that has online video capability as well as presentation and white board options to further student interactions and demonstrations. If your computer does not have a video camera, most are sold separately and come with a companion disc to instruct you on usability. If you don't have a headset complete with microphone, volume control, and muting options, pick one up. A wireless headset is optional if you don't mind dealing with batteries or remembering to charge your device, but if you tend to be very busy, a simple USB headset works just fine.

Now that your hardware is in place, let's review some of the software requirements. Most computers come with a few essential programs, such as the latest browser upgrades and antivirus software, but if that is all you have on your system, you may need to invest in a few additional programs. Whether you are attending college in class or online, you will eventually face the challenge of writing, and the higher your degree level, the more taxing the writing projects become. Investing in a writing program such as MS Word is useful to assist with spell-check, grammar correction recommendations, and formatting. There are also a number of templates you can use if needed. Because you will dabble a bit in presentation development, Microsoft Office is an easy way to go; it covers most educational corners. Microsoft Office includes a combination of Word for writing, PowerPoint for presentation development, Excel for statistics, Access for relational database development, and Outlook for e-mail.

And last, it seems just about everybody has a smartphone these days. Although they can be distracting at times, smartphones can be a great convenience due to the number of free apps available to assist with a variety of student needs, such as eBooks and scheduling applications (apps). If you are juggling a number of classes, scheduling apps will become your next best friend. In addition, most universities that offer online courses also have a university app. University apps offer the capability to check discussion boards or announcements from instructors, view statuses on submitted assignments, or view university e-mail.

If you have these simple basics covered, you are better prepared to face your first quarter without the added pressure of learning technology tools. One last word of advice: become very familiar with your university website. There are valuable time savers available to students, such as online tutors, citation developers, plagiarism detectors, and a wealth of referenced materials located in the university library. It may seem like a large amount to take on even before your class begins, but when fall quarter arrives, you will be way ahead of your classmates.

Plagiarism Detectors

A student has just arrived home after a late night out with friends and needs to wake up early the next morning to attend an important meeting. Oh no: a research paper for the MBA Business Intelligence class is due online before midnight? Exhausted and in no condition to concentrate on writing a research paper, the student glances at the "CTRL" and "C" keys on the keyboard and copies an article from the Internet, then uses the "CTRL" and "V" keys to paste it onto a blank document file. "Who's going to know?" the student thinks.

Plagiarism is the act of stealing and using the words or ideas of another as your own. In other words, plagiarism is cheating. Whether you are writing an article or book, creating a presentation for work, or conducting research for a school paper, plagiarism is a serious act with serious consequences. Due to the vast amount of knowledge available on the Internet today, plagiarism is one of the greatest temptations for college students.

There are various types of plagiarism; the most common types are:

- **Cloning:** using another person's words verbatim.

- **Paraphrasing:** expressing another person's words or ideas without providing cited sources.

- **Poor Quoting:** using quotes around partial sections of paraphrased work, but not in its entirety. All paraphrased work must have quotes around it, or the source be cited within the paraphrased work.

- **Paraphrasing Remix:** using a variety of paraphrases and remixing the order to make it appear as if it is your original work.

- **Self Plagiarism:** using one's previous class assignment for a different class assignment.

Educational institutions take plagiarism seriously and are unforgiving when determining the best course of action against those who decide to plagiarize. If caught, the student can receive no credit for the assignment, receive a failing grade for the course, be suspended, or be expelled. Many distance-learning university programs will require students to review a plagiarism learning module to ensure they fully understand the act of plagiarism and the consequences involved. To alleviate any temptation you may have to take the plagiarism path, keep in mind that identifying plagiarized work is as easy as the act of plagiarism itself.

There are many free, online plagiarism checkers and detectors available. The user simply copies the text from the college paper and pastes it within the plagiarism detector and voilà; you will either get a "thumbs up" or "thumbs down." Use the key words "plagiarism detector" or "plagiarism checker" or "plagiarism apps" on your web browser to learn more. Most universities have their own advanced plagiarism detectors that also display web characters in research papers to determine if work has been copied.

These days, technology benefits both the student and the instructor, creating a more even playing field. The best method around plagiarism is to write using your own thoughts and words. The work will be original, fresh, and you'll feel much better about receiving high marks knowing you did your own writing.

Student eBooks

There is no denying that achieving a college education can be very expensive, and when full-time students physically attend universities far from home, they can expect hefty bills each year. In addition to the usual expenses, such as books, supplies, a laptop, a printer, and a phone, they can also expect to pay for daily living expenses, including meals, clothes, furniture, transportation, and entertainment. Due to the fluctuating economic conditions of the past several years, building up a nest egg to pay for a college education can be a bit of a challenge. There are several ways students can reduce college expenses. One way is to buy eBooks (aka digital books) instead of print-version textbooks for university courses.

Thanks to the invention of the tablet and e-readers, students can now invest in these affordable handheld devices to accommodate their many personal and educational needs. One benefit that tablets and e-readers offer is the ability to download e-books, which are offered at a much reduced price compared to new print-version textbooks. Benefits of purchasing e-books are that they download in a matter of minutes, they weigh nothing, and they are always available as long as students carry their tablets. Standard digital features of e-books include hyperlinked references, instant vocabulary definitions by simply clicking on a word, and highlighting capabilities. Users can even print out e-book sections. Most e-books also have search capabilities as well as sharing options to be used with social media tools.

Two of the most common complaints about e-readers and tablets are eye strain and battery life. Significant eye strain is often associated with long-term reading using tablets and e-readers, particularly on devices with bright back lighting. Users can minimize eye strain by stepping away from their e-books each hour to rest their eyes. Some e-readers and tablets have options for changing the back-light brightness to lower settings; adjusting the screen's brightness can also help users avoid eye strain. Another complaint is the longevity of e-reader and tablet batteries. Depending on the type of device purchased, the user may need to charge the battery regularly to ensure access to the e-books.

Because this is a relatively new option for college students, availability of all university textbooks in the e-book format is somewhat limited. When an e-book version is not available, another option is to purchase the used version of a textbook. Depending on the condition of the used textbook, the university may be willing to purchase the book back at a reduced cost. With new textbooks, the buy-back options are usually quite good, and some universities even offer a pre-paid mailing label to print out and attach to the return package. Students can research university websites to learn more about book buy-back options.

Mind Mapping Tools

Inevitably, at some point in life, you will experience some form of writer's block. Creating beginning and ending concepts for a story or research paper may seem simple, but when it's time to actually begin writing, you suddenly fail to recall all of those great ideas you thought of earlier in the day. To collect ideas that may pop into your head during various times, carry a pocket-size notebook and pen, or, better yet, use your cell phone to record your ideas. These are habits you can practice to capture spur-of-the-moment thoughts, but to transform these ideas into a paper that flows well you will still have to create an outline; this is where mind maps come in handy.

Mind maps provide a visual that represents your thought process. Using this bird's-eye-view technique is a great way to identify holes in the initial structure of your story or research paper. A good analogy for understanding how mind maps work is to think about your thought process when you're surfing the web. How many times have you sat down to look up a particular subject only to find yourself reading something completely unrelated a few minutes later? This happens because there are key words in the initial site that grab your attention and shift your state of mind to another topic. The result is that you end up navigating to the next webpage associated with that new topic. If you looked at a graphic image of the architectural structure of the World Wide Web, you would be looking at something incredibly similar to a mind map. Writing stories or research papers can use this same process.

Developing a mind map is a fun activity; here's how it works. You can either use a large sheet of paper and colored markers, a graphics program, or a mind map application. Begin by drawing a circle in the middle of your canvas of choice. Within the circle, write a word or phrase indicative of the central topic of your paper. Next, draw a line from that circle, and attach another circle to the end of that line. Write a subtopic in the new circle, and continue creating new circles until you run out of ideas.

Mind maps are great for solving writer's block, but they can also be used for other purposes, such as for visually presenting information or ideas, planning, problem solving, brainstorming, group collaborating, teaching, learning, or note taking during a meeting. A mind map is a great way to help an audience understand your thought process. Mind maps can not only help students improve their writing abilities, but they can also improve brainstorming and collaboration within a work environment.

On the next page is an example of a mind map created during the initial thought process for this article.

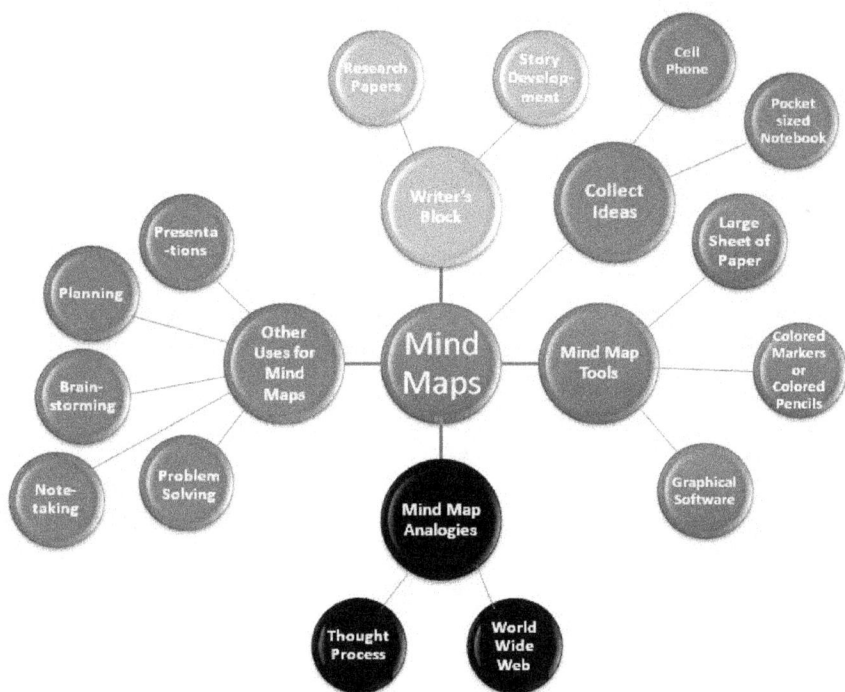

Online Tutors

At some point in your academic life, the need for a tutor will likely arise, and whether you decide to enlist the assistance of a tutor is a personal choice. However, using the services of a tutor is not something most students are comfortable announcing to their friends; as a matter of fact, some students are simply embarrassed by the fact that they need a tutor.

But personal tutors or tutoring services can not only help you improve your grade but also provide you with a variety of techniques to assist in learning and thoroughly understanding the fundamentals of your material. Tutors help you stay on track if you use one throughout the duration of your program. Using a tutor broadens your scope of learning. There are some tutoring services available on campus to students who physically attend universities, or the university website should have a tutoring resource available for virtual students to use. Depending on the university you are attending, some of the tutoring services are offered to students free of charge. One popular online tutoring service is called Smarthinking.

Smarthinking offers seasoned educators with advanced degrees an opportunity to help the learner be the best student possible. Students can schedule an appointment ahead of time to meet with a tutor for 30-minute tutoring sessions. Smarthinking tutors are available 24 hours a day, 7 days a week, and they will meet one on one with the student using real-time communication technology. The tutoring sessions are recorded and archived so, if needed, students can review them at a later date.

Smarthinking offers tutoring in a variety of subjects, such as reading, business, mathematics, English for speakers of other languages, science,

Spanish, nursing and allied health, computer technology, and writing. Many advanced degrees require writing assignments to be error free in grammar and mechanics. Additionally, bibliographies are required for each advanced-degree research paper and must follow the appropriate writing style assigned, for example, Modern Language Association (MLA), American Psychological Association (APA), and Chicago Documentation Style (CMOS). The Smarthinking online writing lab allows students to submit their papers ahead of time for tutors to review and critique in a relatively short turnaround time.

Once students decide to enlist the services of Smarthinking tutors, they can expect the following services: constructive criticism, assistance with identifying problem areas, and strategies to help them better understand their particular areas of study. However, Smarthinking will not complete the assignments for the distance learner, provide answers, correct errors, or predict a possible grade outcome. Smarthinking is a tutoring service, and the tutors collaborate with the learners to provide them with the personal guidance needed to make them better students.

Citing Sources for Research Papers

Every college student will inevitably need to write a college-level research paper at some point in his or her academic journey, particularly after reaching the master's or doctoral level. As interesting as these studies may be, the challenge of utilizing an appropriate citation format will present a hurdle students will face on a regular basis.

A citation can be a quotation or alphanumeric expression contained within the body of your paper that identifies a piece of literature taken from an external source used within your paper. Citing work is a way to substantiate your view on a topic by using empirical evidence another has uncovered on the same subject matter.

Many citations share the same basic components such as author name, title of article, publication date, place of publication, and publisher. Depending on the institution you attend and the discipline you study, you will encounter specific citation formats you must use. Citation style guides can be found as published books, online, and on your university library website. Three popular citation styles are as follows:

- **American Psychological Association (APA)** is a professional and scientific organization for psychologists.

- **Modern Language Association (MLA)** is a professional association composed of professors, graduate students, and academic scholars.

- **The Chicago Manual of Style (CMS)**, published at the University of Chicago Press, focuses on editorial practice in English grammar, document preparation, and history.

Citations are necessary when quoting another person's work. They give credit where credit is due. All resources cited in a research paper should be listed at the end of the research paper in a format called a bibliography (aka references and works cited). Depending on the style guide used, bibliographies can be a cumbersome chore to create, as the order of cited work varies depending on the style used. Historically, student were required to create the list of cited sources themselves, but today with advancement in technology, students can simply use an online interactive web tool that creates the citations for you. You simply fill out the online form, select the style guide preference, and voilà; the citations appear in appropriate bibliographic format. Nevertheless, not all websites claiming to create citations in the appropriate format produce accurate service. To ensure that your citations are in the correct format, always be certain to keep a style guide pocketbook close by or check your university website to see if it offers a bibliography, reference, or citation generator.

PATRICIA PEDRAZA-NAFZIGER

LEARNING METHODOLOGIES
AND RESOURCES

Fundamentals for the
Distance Learning Student

After several years in a career that fails to meet your satisfaction, you begin contemplating an advanced degree to broaden your opportunities. However, it has been a number of years since you last attended college, and you are beginning to feel a little anxious about sitting in a classroom filled with younger students. You have considered distance learning, but are not sure you can keep up with the technology that may be involved in online courses. A person must consider several factors before making the decision to participate in a distance learning program to determine if it is the right choice for their lifestyle and goals.

Time management is one of the key qualities needed for distance learning. Online students must be able to manage a daily schedule. As a distance learner, you will have access to your entire course schedule once the course begins. Plan a daily study schedule to ensure you do not get behind. There are calendar and scheduling apps available to help you manage your time. Procrastination is one of the worst habits a distance learning student can have, so, if you procrastinate, you are less likely to complete your distance learning course successfully.

Demanding lifestyles are pretty common among distance learning students, which is one of the reasons they choose to learn in a virtual setting. By attending a distance learning institution, students can save commuting time and schedule their own study sessions. Because your life is already challenging enough, you may want to consider beginning with a simple three-credit course to test the waters. This is a great way to determine if you have the time to complete your coursework on schedule before wholly committing to a distance learning program.

Reading proficiency is necessary for distance learners. In lieu of listening to classroom lectures, you will be required to read lecture material online in addition to your normal coursework reading. This can be a time-consuming effort if reading is not your forte. Another consideration if you suffer from eye strain from overusing your computer at work is that you must spend additional time in front of the computer to complete your coursework at home.

Writing skills are a must for any distance learner. If you have decided to pursue a distance learning education but do not consider your writing up to college standards, sign up for a few writing classes before you begin. This will provide you with the momentum you need to begin your distance learning program. If you do sign up for writing classes, take them online so that you can test whether or not you enjoy the distance learning environment.

Basic computer skills will get you through the fundamentals of distance learning. Do you have at least basic computer skills? Ensure you have the necessary equipment prior to getting started in your distance learning program. A brief review of some of the basic essentials will be covered later.

Independent work is a must. You may have questions about the coursework at times when your instructor is not available. It is during times such as these that you must make vital decisions regarding your coursework. Distance learners are expected to work independently to solve problems without the immediate support you get from a teacher in onsite classes.

Self-motivation is a daily chore. There are always times you would rather do things other than studying. It is important to review your coursework at the beginning of the week to ensure you allocate enough time throughout each day to fulfill the course requirements. At the beginning of each week, taking a sneak peek at your weekly requirements can help you out. Realizing what is due will linger in the back of your mind as a constant reminder of what you should be doing.

Distance learning can be a rewarding experience, equal to and perhaps even greater than education in a traditional classroom environment. Knowing the basic requirements ahead of time will give you the jump start needed to create a smooth journey throughout your distance learning experience.

The Importance of Writing Skills

Writing is considered one of the most important transferrable skills for employees to possess. The quality of writing is what first captures a job recruiter's attention and helps determine your qualifications. As distance learners, students are continually adapting and improving their writing skills because it is their main avenue for communicating with fellow students and instructors, whereas in a classroom environment, verbal communication is typically used.

For some, writing is a normal process that comes with ease. The words just seem to come naturally and flow with perfect grammar and clarity. For others, it is a real struggle. Many find writing to be like a puzzle in which the rules of grammar are confusing, finding the right words to represent intended meanings is a difficult task, and assembling the flow of words for an idea becomes frustrating. The fact remains, some individuals find writing papers as challenging as others find math problems.

Ensuring that your quality of writing is up to par for a job search is vital. When drafting a resume, cover letter, and personal statement, if you lack confidence in your writing ability, it is always wise to have a second pair of eyes review the documents prior to submission. If you are friends with an English teacher or editor, approach them about your concerns, and ask them to review the document and make recommendations for improvements. Another alternative, if you have the means, is to hire an editing service. There are many reasons people hire editing services, and there is no reason to be ashamed to do so. Your ultimate goal is to project the best first impression possible, so the small investment you make for an editing service is likely to be money well spent.

Thanks to the evolution of information technology, there are many editing services available online today. One such editing service is called ProofreadingPal. It is a valuable resource that provides professional editing to help tailor your resume, curriculum vitae, academic research papers, manuscripts, or business documents. The professional editors review your documents for punctuation and grammatical errors, sentence structure, and flow. You are charged per word, and the turnaround time is flexible, anywhere from 90 minutes to 5 days, depending on how much you would like to invest.

Another alternative you may want to consider is utilizing the university library or tutoring services for editing purposes. Some universities offer editing services free of charge as long as you are enrolled for a course at the time of the service. Unlike professional editing services, university online tutors will provide you with suggestions for improvements within the document rather than making the edits for you. You can modify the document and submit it back several times until you get it right; this may be the best option for learning purposes. Either way, ensuring your documents are error free is a great way to make a good first impression.

To learn more visit **Proofreadingpal.com**, or your university website.

Developing a
Critical-Thinking Mindset

No matter what level of education people achieve, chances are they have, or will eventually come across, the term "critical thinking." Critical thinking is a process in which an individual questions the reasoning behind a particular claim or decision. As complicated as critical thinking may sound, it is a thought process that most people already use on a small scale to make important decisions about their families, careers, or finances. For example, purchasing a new car is not a decision to be taken lightly. There are many factors to consider, such as want versus need, affordability, cost of insurance, gas mileage, safety, reliability, new versus pre-owned, and so on. Thoroughly researching and evaluating each factor prior to drawing a conclusion is utilizing critical thinking.

Conversely, critical thinking draws on a more complex and integrated practice during an educational journey, particularly when people begin to reach graduate-level coursework. In academics, critical thinking can be defined as using reasoning to broaden perspectives on knowledge presented, whether it's in a book, research on the Internet, a lecture, or a discussion. Questioning the reasoning behind the information is the first step in the critical-thinking process. People must be critical of any information presented. They must practice skepticism and understand the reasoning behind assumptions rather than simply accepting an answer. Employing this practice not only broadens people's understanding, it heightens learning and develops a mindset that is better suited for problem solving. To help establish a critical thinking mindset, people should ponder the following questions when drawing conclusions:

- What questions arise about the data?

- What are the key assumptions?

- Does the argument seem vague in its conclusion?

- Is there a contradiction in any of the data?

- Is the data justifiable?

- Is the view biased?

- Is there data to oppose the position as well as to support it?

Reasoning is the operative word behind the critical-thinking process. Simply defined, reasoning is an individual's ability to make sense of things, to be open to new knowledge and facts despite personal beliefs, and to utilize those facts or new knowledge to help establish conclusions. The process of critical thinking becomes more complex as people progress into higher levels of coursework; consequently, it is vital that they establish the skill of critical thinking early in their academic journeys.

Virtual Communication
and Learning

Distance learning has been around for a long time, and even though course work requirements tend to be similar for both distance learning and classroom instruction, communication methods have changed. Recently, corporations are beginning to rethink the benefits of providing their employees the option of working virtually because recent studies indicate communicating and knowledge sharing in a virtual environment are less effective than in a face-to-face environment. Are we living in a world where increased mobile technology is actually starting to hinder communication?

Face-to-face communication and learning can differ from virtual communication and learning. Some university instructors use a large movie theater–type classroom environment to conduct their lectures, which is less likely to encourage feedback compared to classrooms with fewer students where interaction is often encouraged. Conversely, in a virtual learning environment, feedback from fellow students on discussion assignments is required to receive a minimum passing grade. Virtual communication can be just as effective, if not more so, because of the fact that students have time to ponder their thoughts and thoroughly compose their views for other students to comment on.

Below is a list of benefits and challenges students face when choosing between learning in a traditional classroom environment versus a virtual online learning environment.

Traditional Classroom Learning Environment:

- Face-to-face classroom environment

- Room designed and furnished to provide optimal learning space, closed and free of outside distractions

- Limited time frame for hours of instruction

- Diversity limited to local student participation

- Classroom environment imposes accountability

- Students motivated to stay alert, concerned about what the teacher will think

- Teachers are better positioned to motivate and inspire students

- Extroverts thrive in this environment

- Introverts are hindered in this environment

- Verbal feedback on topics usually involves only a few brave souls

- Student projects are often fostered in a group environment

- Traditional classroom takes more time

Virtual Online Learning Environment:

- Any online area where instructors and students meet for course activities

- Virtual learning space could be more distracting if designated area is not established

- Students tend to be located in different states, sometimes different countries, which encourages diverse interaction

- Knowledge of virtual collaboration tools and computer equipment is necessary

- Open for operation 24/7

- Virtual environment teaches students how to work independently

- Virtual classroom saves time, especially for working individuals or full-time caretakers

- Students need to learn to be self-motivated

- Students learn the importance of time management

- Writing discussions are required in every class if you want to pass; student writing abilities improve

- Students find it easier to seek assistance from fellow students in a virtual setting

- Students are free to brainstorm their own theories, which fosters creativity

Netiquette and
Discussion Board Etiquette

Netiquette, commonly known as online etiquette, is a social code for network communication, which outlines behavioral expectations when communicating or collaborating with others online, via e-mail, in chat rooms, or on discussion boards. Students who participate in distance-learning classes typically correspond with one another using discussion boards or chat rooms made available to them through their university websites. Just as first impressions are made when individuals meet face-to-face for the first time, so can similar impressions be made based on your first online interactions.

Typically, when you first initiate your online university course, the very first assignment is to introduce yourself to other online students participating on the same discussion board. A brief description of who you are, where you're from, your educational background, current occupation, and what you hope to accomplish by taking the course is generally what is expected in your introduction. However, you can also personalize your introduction by sharing interests, such as hobbies, family travels, pets, and just providing a little bit of information about your personal background (while, of course, using your discretion). This can transform your introduction from a first assignment into an engaging correspondence.

While communicating and collaborating with others on a university discussion board, please be aware that your audience could be comprised of a variety of age groups and cultures. The type of language used should always be respectful and considerate of others' values. University discussion boards are a great way to learn from fellow students and to share the knowledge and experience you have with others. Communications between students located around the world can broaden students' ways of thinking simply by exposing them to how other generations or cultures may view things differently from how they view them.

In an academic environment, it is always wise to utilize appropriate language free of online chat abbreviations, including LOL, OMG, 2MORO, BTW, BFN, ETA, FYI, TTYL, BCNU, GR8, etc. Save the shorthand for your text messages or personal social media communications. Other common conventions associated with university netiquette are ensuring your work is spell-checked before submitting it, trying to avoid "ALL CAPS" during discussion (it is perceived as shouting), being honest, refraining from "flaming" (insulting others), being conservative in the language you use, and, most of all, being yourself. And when you're not in an academic environment, always be aware that the information you choose to share in cyberspace can never be considered private again, so be sure you understand the environment you are about to delve into before you do so.

Social Learning Online

Social media provides virtual communities as a means of networking to create, share, and exchange user-generated content with others. Social media is an interactive web-based platform available via computers and mobile devices with real-time results. The popularity of social media includes high school and college students communicating and collaborating on a regular daily basis, with the generation of Baby Boomers following along. Even seniors are starting to embrace social media as a way to stay in touch with family and friends. Aside from using social media to manage social life interactions, social media can also be used as a method of learning, aka social learning, and is a great way to cater to all learning styles and personalities. Two of the most popular social media websites today are **Facebook** and **YouTube**.

Facebook is an online social media site to help students become acquainted with one another. Originating at Harvard University as an academic social networking tool, it has now branched out globally and has become the most popular social media website known today. Facebook is being used by many university professors as a means to communicate and collaborate with students outside the classroom and as a method for students in similar disciplines to collaborate on long-term projects. The "group" feature allows circles of people to share information on specific educational topics, such as learning opportunities, writing dissertations, educational scholarship organizations, and educational networking in general. Group accounts also have the option of having an open or closed forum, depending on privacy requirements. Facebook can be used as a great companion tool for educators and students worldwide.

Created by three former PayPal employees in 2005, YouTube is a video-sharing website that allows users to upload, view, share, and comment on videos. Videos shared range from music to sports, gaming, movies, TV shows, and news. There are also videos for learning. Depending on the topic of choice (e.g., math, philosophy, psychology, computing, you name it), the YouTube search engine will provide a list of results ranging from actual lectures from top universities to step-by-step explanations of how to solve an equation or helpful tips on writing a dissertation proposal. The learning opportunities are endless—and for some, observational learning enhances their learning outcome.

The format of distance learning is evolving; from computer-based learning to internet-based learning, social learning seems to be the next phase of the learning evolution. By using social media as another dimension for learning, students not only learn, they learn by interacting with peers in an environment that feels casual, which is a great foundation for cultivating relationships and teamwork.

Wikipedia for
College Research

At some point during your academic journey, you will be required to write a research paper in which you thoroughly explore a particular subject, cite sources in a detailed bibliography, and format the paper in appropriate MLA, APA, or other required university style. In the past two decades, resources for research have vastly improved. Instead of making a trip to the library and dedicating several hours to scanning through microfiche or flipping through card catalogs, you can now browse the web on your mobile device in the comfort of your own home or a local coffee shop. The convenience of researching has improved immensely, but the vortex of data now available at your fingertips complicates the simple task of searching for a credible source.

Using the local public library or university library for research is a great way to ensure the data you find is reliable, but if you locate resources on the Internet, how do you know the validity of the material? Anybody can publish data on the Internet; Wikipedia is a perfect example of this. Wikipedia is an online encyclopedia of data authored by individuals from around the world who use this free, collaborative environment to share knowledge with one another. Unfortunately, the accuracy of the data shared on Wikipedia is only as reliable as the author providing the data. Since this collaborative knowledge-sharing environment welcomes anonymous authors and shared editing, assessing the validity of the data is a time-consuming process. Some amount of inaccurate information is inevitably shared.

Despite the inaccuracy, some professors will not discourage college students from using Wikipedia because it is a great resource for locating cited references. For example, if you are required to write a research paper on the subject of social media, Wikipedia provides a search capability similar to a search engine. You simply type in the key words "social media," and an indexed array of knowledge is displayed, beginning with the definition of social media and followed by entries on the classifications of social media, mobile social media, distinction from other media, criticisms, patents, and so on. An index of content is provided, making it easier for the researcher to navigate through the site. The references section displays 58 cited sources as well as a Further Reading section, which lists publications about social media. From a researcher's perspective, this references section is an ideal way to locate reliable resources that can be used in a university research paper.

But how does the researcher know for sure a cited source is reliable? Every research paper is accompanied by a bibliography that provides details about the sources cited, such as author name, title, publishing company, publication date, and editor just to name a few. When searching the web for references to help substantiate the argument of your research paper, make it a habit to avoid using the first quote you find, and spend a little time searching a variety of articles on the same subject. This should narrow it down to a reliable source your professor will approve of.

HEALTH AND EDUCATION

Exercise and Learning

We have all heard how regular exercise can contribute to better health and fitness, but the benefits of a good workout can also improve your mood, memory, concentration, and intellect. Exercise can be defined as a physical activity used to promote muscle exertion. The human body was meant to move and be active, a need that dates back to the time when people had to hunt for and gather their own food in order to survive. During your exercise routine, you will notice your need for oxygen increases, as does your heart rate. You begin to perspire, and your muscles may actually feel pain, depending on the type of exercise in which you engage. This process helps your body's performance and slows down the aging process.

The brain is similar to our muscles and organs because its performance and functionality decline rapidly if not used. However, studies show that exercise will reduce this rate of decline, and even develop new brain cells, also called neurons, which have a short shelf life if not used. These newly generated brain cells are floating around waiting to network with other brain cells, and learning is the key that allows them to network with one another. To put it simply: Exercise + Learning = Improved Intellect.

Although technology has afforded the convenience and mobility that many of us desire, it has also contributed to the lack of physical activity from which many of us suffer. Day after day we sit behind our computers to work, to attend school, and even to network and socialize. Additionally, during our leisure time we sit in front of the television for pleasure and relaxation. Today, with all the sedentary distractions we have in our daily lives, finding time to exercise can be a challenge.

Maintaining a regular workout schedule should be as high on your priority list as scheduling meetings for work, taking your kids to school, or completing college research papers. Exercising your heart and body is essential for overall wellness and improved mental performance.

Maintaining one's concentration or focus can be challenging at times, whether you are a child, young adult, middle-ager, or a senior citizen, concentration and focus require effort. Studies show those who performed better on fitness tests also have a tendency to score higher on concentration tests. Do you know if you are getting enough exercise each week? There are a variety of recommendations that dictate the amount of exercise it takes to live a healthy lifestyle. The time you dedicate to an exercise program is important, but it is equally important to mix up your workout routine. Incorporating walking, weight training, stretching, and a cardio option, such as dance or aerobics, into your weekly routine will allow different muscles to work at various times, which is better for you in the long term. No matter on which options you decide, just remember you're not only improving your physical fitness and health, you're improving your mind.

Smart Foods for Brain Health

There is an old saying: "You are what you eat." What exactly does that mean? You might just as easily say the opposite: "You are what you don't eat." There are differences between the types of foods you eat to provide energy to the body and the foods you eat to provide energy to the brain. I am a virtual student who is constantly striving to stay focused, and foods that encourage concentration and enhance memory are always first on my list of things to help me get through the week.

There are many food options to help stimulate brain activity. Let's say you've managed to procrastinate studying for your final or writing a research paper and find yourself overwhelmed by the challenge of catching up after staying up late the night before. The most popular beverages students reach for to get a quick energy fix are those loaded with caffeine. There are several energy drinks available, but caffeine can also be found in chocolate. Although they offer a quick fix for a tired mind, these options also contain an abundance of sugar, providing you with an instant high, which can actually make it more difficult to concentrate. Further, they often leave you with a headache and a feeling of fatigue once the effect has worn off.

Your best options to help you stay awake are tea or coffee—not a high-sugar latte, but a cup or two of coffee or tea with a little sweetener and fat-free cream, if needed. Although sugar does have effects that run counter to stimulating concentration, there are some natural sugar alternatives that can quickly arouse your brain activity. Fruits, such as apples and oranges, can provide just enough natural sugar to provide a quick energy boost, much like coffee does. Eating an apple or orange can also provide your body with the necessary fiber, vitamins, and nutrients it needs on a daily basis.

Foods associated with long-term benefits to brain health are those high in omega-3 fatty acids, which contribute to improved memory as we age. The following are foods high in omega-3 fatty acids:

- **Nuts and Grains:** Nutty or whole wheat breads, flaxseeds, oatmeal, flour tortillas, and peanut butter

- **Seafood:** Salmon, oysters, halibut, trout, and sardines

- **Vegetables:** Broccoli, carrots, bell peppers, mint, parsley, spinach, Brussels sprouts, and soybeans

- **Dairy:** Eggs, yogurt, milk, and margarine

There are also many vitamins you can take to help boost your energy level first thing in the morning, but the best brain booster option to start your day is to eat a healthy, well-rounded breakfast filled with grains, protein, and fruits. You should eat only until satisfied; otherwise, too full a tummy could make you drowsy. Studies have shown that students who eat a good breakfast perform better academically compared to those who choose to skip breakfast. So try to make time in your busy schedule to consume the necessary fuel your mind and body need to allow you to perform at your physical and mental best!

How to Manage
Student Stress

Attending college full time requires a bit of adaptation when it comes to managing your time, and part-time college students with full-time jobs and families can experience a great deal of stress in their daily lives. Stress has a tendency to sneak up on you without your even realizing it is there. Stress is a feeling to which we start to become accustomed. So, how do you know you're stressed? Some of the symptoms associated with stress are:

- Anxiety

- Constant headaches

- Tense or aching muscles, particularly around your shoulders and neck

- Dental issues associated with grinding of the teeth

- Feeling irritated or overwhelmed

- Loss of sexual desire

- Increased use of alcohol

- Pessimistic attitude

- Overeating

- Memory issues

If you are suffering from a number of these symptoms, you may need to take a second look at how you manage stress in your life. Stress is not something to be taken lightly; it is a major factor associated with many illnesses and diseases, such as:

- Insomnia

- Depression

- Diabetes

- High blood pressure

- Heart disease

- Obesity

- Accelerated aging

- Heartburn

Creating a balanced lifestyle is a great way to begin minimizing stresses in your life. Managing your activities and organizing them in a fashion that makes the most of your time is one of the keys to eliminating factors associated with stress. Take a few minutes to write down all the activities in your daily life, and then divide the list into two groups: internal balance and external balance.

The internal balance list items pertain to activities that affect your overall health, heart, and mind. The external balance list items pertain to your family, friends, and career. Having an equal balance between internal and external can greatly contribute to stress reduction. But balancing time is not always an easy task. It is best to utilize some sort of scheduling method to help you manage your time. There are many scheduling apps available for exactly this purpose. Find one that works best for you and begin organizing your daily activities.

While attending college, some of the top reasons students are stressed out have to do with money. To ensure your college experience is a positive one, make sure you are financially prepared. If you are certain that money will be a concern once you begin attending college in the fall, try sacrificing some of your summertime freedom to obtain a job that will work well with your college schedule. It is always best to start to eliminate stresses associated with money early; attending college itself will demand much of your time.

Procrastination is one of the biggest contributors to stress in my life as a student. At the very least, I've learned to designate time once a day to review course material or assignments that are due later in the week. Even if I don't complete the assignment or actually work on it on any given day, reviewing it provides me with fuel for thought. While I'm exercising or cooking, ideas will pop into my head pertaining to the assignment's requirements. Understanding the weekly coursework early on will give you an idea of how to manage your time, which will ultimately help you to better organize your time and to make you a better student.

Time Management

Making the transition from being a classroom student to a distance learning student does require the organization of one's time. Distance learning students choose learning in a virtual setting as a means of convenience for their busy lifestyle. Electronic scheduling systems can be of great benefit when it comes to being a full-time distance learning student or a part-time student who is also working in addition to managing his or her personal life.

First, a distance learner should utilize at least one of the many tools available to schedule and track his or her time. A variety of desk or wall calendars are designed specifically for academic purposes in many office supply stores or online. However, these days mobile students prefer to have their personal, professional, and educational resources available to them at their fingertips via laptops, tablets, or smartphones. Many scheduling applications (apps) are available as a free download for most devices. Typically the free download apps contain limited capabilities. For more advanced applications, one may have to only pay a few dollars, which is a relatively cheap investment for time management assistance. Research the Internet using they key words "schedule apps" to determine what scheduling app is best suited for your lifestyle.

Whatever your schedule preference may be, before beginning each quarter or semester, add the information listed on your university class syllabus for each course, specifically:

- Post the class schedule from beginning to end for each day of the week.

- Post all assignment due dates for each week.

- Post all discussion board due dates.

- If there are comprehensive exams scheduled, try to schedule study time.

- Activate a reminder for each item if you tend to be forgetful.

Managing college classes while juggling your work and personal life can be an acquired skill. Scheduling applications such as Outlook's Scheduler provides a color coding system to help you prioritize your calendar, for example:

- Red = Important

- Green = Personal

- Blue = Travel Required

- Or you can even customize your own coding system by defining what each color means.

Using scheduling tools to assist in organization can save you a great deal of time and frustration. While participating in distance learning programs, you will begin to understand how much time is needed to complete weekly assignments as you proceed through each quarter or semester. Initially, not all college students have the luxury of beginning their degree program by only taking one class per quarter or semester. Many degree programs are designed to be completed within a specific period of time, which means several classes per quarter or semester. The key to being a successful distance learning student is to balance your lifestyle. Using schedule apps to help you prioritize and organize your life is a great first step.

Staying Motivated

With a difficult and long term goal such as a college education it is important to have an incentive to keep you motivated. Whether you're trying to eat healthier, exercise more, or quit smoking, the ultimate goal is improved health and a greater chance for a longer life. Distance Learning students face particular challenges in this respect because they lack the scheduled times to attend class, listen to lectures, complete reading assignments, and participate in discussions. Time management falls entirely on the student, and motivational support is an independent effort. Staying focused on your degree is a great way to maintain motivation, but with all the stresses and distractions surrounding you on a daily basis, keeping focused on what needs to be done is not always an easy task.

By nature, human beings are easily distracted, and today there are an abundance of impediments diverting their attention such as family, work, cell phones, text messages, social media, TV, video games, random thoughts, hunger pains, and simply boredom. Staying focused and motivated to complete your coursework and degree program takes planning. Try removing all distractions before you sit down to begin your study session. Although I'm a huge fan of learning, my lack of desire for completing coursework is apparent. Take a personal example, I find myself trying to complete all my daily tasks before I begin to study, by doing so I've wiped my slate clean leaving nothing in my path to distract my thought process when I finally do attend to my coursework. This process eliminates most distractions, so when I enter my study environment I can dedicate all my attention to my coursework or writing. But don't let yourself turn eliminating distractions into avoiding your work.

Your selected study environment should be one that makes your thought process flourish. Do you have a place where you typically study, a place that allows your ideas to percolate? Individuals thrive in different types of environments. Some prefer the atmosphere of a busy coffee shop, and some the solitude of a quiet room sitting next to a window filled with views that enhance their imagination. This is a very personal choice. Discovering the environment that works best for you is essential, and using that environment on a regular basis will help you develop a routine that will continue to stimulate your motivation.

Completing your weekly coursework is an accomplishment in itself, but sometimes it helps to spice up those accomplishments with a small reward, whether something relaxing or something exciting. For instance, if you have a number of TV shows you record on a weekly basis, postpone viewing them until you've completed your coursework. Perhaps you enjoy playing a round of golf once or twice a week. Plan those tee times after your designated coursework times. Without your schoolwork hanging over your head, a round of golf can then feel like a real reward. Whatever reward you choose as motivation, always try to remember the reasons inspiring you to go to college in the first place. Never forget your degree.

Ergonomics

People who have participated in distance learning programs can tell you how convenient they can be, but for those whose careers require hours and hours in front of their computers, distance learning courses mean the additional strain of being tied to the screen outside of their regularly scheduled work hours as they fulfill course work, listen to lectures, and participate in discussion boards. For those who find themselves in front of the computer for long periods of time, consider investing in some type of computer break software. There are different kinds of computer break applications available as free downloads or for purchase, and the applications meet various needs.

Each application will have specific system requirements. When you find the software that best agrees with your computer, you simply download the software and complete the required user information. **WorkPace** is a good example of a highly effective software used by many large corporations. Anytime the computer boots up, the computer break software will actively run in the background of your computer system, monitoring your daily keyboard and mouse activity. Throughout the day, during study time, work, or leisure, the computer break software will measure whether you've taken adequate breaks. If a given amount of time has passed without taking a break, a pop-up image will notify you that it's time for one. This process continues as the day progresses, and the message will periodically be accompanied by selected exercises to participate in for the specific time allocated. Each exercise break presents a visual image of the exercise routine along with instructions. A few of these ergonomic exercises include:

- Micropause Stretch and Relax

- Lean Back Arm Drop

- Trapezius Stretch

- Change in Focus

- Neck Side Stretches

- Head Turns

- Shoulder Shrugs

- Sitting Trunk Twists

- Blinking

- Arm Shakes

- Back Stretch

- Palm Stretch

- Forward Lean

- Head Back

WorkPace also allows you to select an enforced level of activity ranging from low to high. The enforcement level will permit you to bypass the exercises for an unlimited amount of time (low level) or not allow you to ignore the commands (high level). If you completely ignore the designated breaks that you originally preprogrammed, your keyboard will automatically be disabled for the break's designated time. WorkPace also offers statistical data related to the start and end times of computer use, right- and left-hand keyboard strokes, and number of mouse clicks or double clicks.

By following the commands of your WorkPace application, you will improve concentration and productivity, reduce the effects of fatigue and discomfort, and avoid the eye strain that is so commonly associated with long-term computer use. Keep in mind that taking a break from your computer to reduce eye strain does not mean stepping away from your workstation to read a smartphone or tablet. If the provided exercises are not appealing, take a short walk, enjoy the view outside, or simply lie down and close your eyes for five or ten minutes. To learn more about the various computer break applications available, type the key words "ergonomic software" or "computer break software" into your browser. And remember: don't forget to take a break while searching.

Computer Vision Syndrome and Eyestrain

It is a commonly known fact that heavy computer use can be a bit of a strain on your eyes, but as a distance learning student, eyestrain is a problem that should not be ignored. Many distance learning students work full time while attending college, and some work in occupations that require heavy computer use. A number of computer software programs are available to remind you to take breaks on occasion to complete ergonomic exercises as well as to rest your eyes. Unfortunately, many users under a deadline simply choose to ignore the "take a break" message. Familiarizing yourself with the warning signs of eyestrain may be a good first step in taking better care of your eyes.

Using various types of electronic devices such as laptops, tablets, smart phones, and personal computers for long periods of time can contribute to eyestrain, also known as computer vision syndrome, which can ultimately affect your work performance and ability to concentrate. Many symptoms are associated with computer vision syndrome, including back, neck, or shoulder pain; dry or watery eyes; sensitivity to light; tired or itchy eyes; difficulty focusing; and blurred vision. Long-term computer vision syndrome is not considered life threatening, but avoiding treating the symptoms could lead to blurred vision and headaches.

Developing practices to take better care of your eyes can help reduce computer vision syndrome. Ensure the lighting in both your workplace and home office is not overbearing and that your computer is not facing a direct source of sunlight, which can create a glare on the screen. Adjust your computer monitor's settings to reduce the brightness level and increase the font size; these adjustments will help reduce extra visual effort. Another form of eyestrain is called focus fatigue. Focus fatigue is caused by staring at the same distance for long periods of time, such as at a computer monitor or at the road while driving. Try stepping away from your computer and observing an object at a longer distance for short periods of time, say 20 seconds. Then shift your eyes to something very close for the same period of time. This eye exercise will help reduce the symptoms of focus fatigue.

If you suffer from computer vision syndrome, ensure you are using the appropriate eyewear. Using prescription reading glasses is great for reading books, but you might consider prescription computer glasses if you are a heavy computer user. Computer glasses have lenses that are designed specifically for the distance between your computer monitor and your eyes. They tend to have a broader visual scope and are sometimes tinted to reduce glare. Computer glasses are for computer use only, not for driving or reading. Although computer glasses can be sold over the counter, please resist the temptation of this convenience and schedule an appointment with your eye doctor. Before your appointment, be sure to measure the distance from your eyes to your computer screen when sitting behind your computer. Purchasing a pair of prescription computer glasses is a worthwhile investment; these glasses will help reduce the effects of eyestrain, which will improve your work performance and concentration.

PATRICIA PEDRAZA-NAFZIGER

FREE DISTANCE LEARNING COURSES

Free Open Courses
at Top Universities

Let's face it: the convenience provided by advancements in technology is only one reason students and universities are turning to distance learning. The elderly do not have to drive to class, and the middle aged population has little time to spare due to family and job obligations. While students of these generations were required to physically attend class, listen to lectures provided by their teachers, and participate in classroom discussions face-to-face, Generation Z students, also known as Millennials, have been exposed to an abundance of knowledge available at their fingertips and expect to network and learn from others outside of the traditional classroom environment.

These digital natives (born between 1994 and 2004) depend on web technologies and mobile devices to stay in touch with friends and family, attend classes, and even network for job opportunities. They have become accustomed to staying mobile and connected. Additionally, while education is important to the Millennial student, investing in advanced degrees is no longer the ultimate goal, particularly for those students who have witnessed their parents struggle to keep their heads above water as they pay for their mortgage, student loans, and living expenses in a declining economic environment.

Today, students are seeking alternative educational avenues that allow them to broaden their higher-learning experiences at a lower cost. For example, there are top universities such as Harvard and MIT that offer free, open online-learning courses in various areas of study. Students who attend walk away with a certificate but no official college credit. Millennial students are completely satisfied with this educational resource and consider the benefits of the knowledge gained to be more relevant than the actual college credit itself.

There are many open courseware resources available:

- OpenUW offers courses in the American Civil War, Greek mythology, and Shakespeare's comedies.

- Open Yale Courses explores astronomy, history, and chemistry.

- Coursera has partnered with 33 universities, including Princeton, Brown, Stanford, Columbia, Duke, and Rice, and has offered 211 free courses in 20 different categories.

- MIT OpenCourseware (OCW) has provided up to 650 online courses from top universities.

- Carnegie Mellon University is an Open Learning Initiative Project offering a variety of courses for next-generation learning.

Top universities are offering these free online courses as a way to measure and better understand the popularity of attending courses online. Although top universities offer online certificate programs, there are much fewer options for achieving an official degree online. As the popularity of these free courses continues to increase, so may the options for achieving online degrees, including advanced degrees from top universities.

University of Washington
OPENUW

Today, students of all ages are seeking alternative educational methods that allow them to broaden their higher-learning experiences at a lower cost. **The University of Washington's OpenUW** offers free online courses at no cost to the student, the only investment you make is time.

The courses offered are similar to those that on-campus students must pay tuition to attend. The only difference is that instead of earning traditional college credits, online students only receive a certificate of completion. For instance, Introduction to Product Management is similar to taking an accredited project management course in many ways. It provides a basic overview including course goals and objectives, course structure, learning modules, supplemental reading material, quizzes, and a project activity.

Each learning module is presented via a narrated slide show that requires the use of computer speakers or headphones. Each quiz includes a list of several true or false questions and an option for time limits, due dates, and availability. For the first project activity, students select a project they are already working on or planning. They must then meet the following goals and answer the following questions:

- Deliverability: What will you accomplish with this project?

- Duration: How long will it take to complete this project?

- Resource assignment: What resources are required to complete this project?

- Original set of tasks: What tasks need to be completed?

- One-time group endeavor: Will you be able to meet your goals in one event?

The subsequent activities assigned continue to build upon students' project goals. Essentially, when the project management course is complete, students walk away with a thorough understanding of the basic concepts required to develop a well thought-out project plan of their own.

OpenUW offers an eclectic span of free, general-interest courses such as Energy, Diet & Weight; HTML Basics; War and History; Dance; Political Economy; and The Study of Personality. The University of Washington also offers more advanced free courses via Coursera in areas that include finance, computational neuroscience, data science, programming languages, machine learning, and a variety of computer-related courses.

Carnegie Mellon University

Carnegie Mellon University is one of a number of top universities offering free online courses through a program called **Open Learning Initiative (OLI)**. OLI's initiative is to provide quality education fueled by continual feedback and research to improve the learning process, which ultimately benefits students, educators, and academic institutions. Founded in 2002, the Carnegie Mellon Open Learning Initiative has integrated its expertise in cognitive tutoring, an intelligent tutoring system, into its first four online courses: Statistics, Logic and Proofs, Casual and Statistical Reasoning, and Economics.

Courses are provided using a web-based instruction method collecting data on student activities that instructors can monitor. The collected data provides a quantitative analysis of learning results for course designers and learning science researchers to review and improve upon. In essence, this process helps the university test specific learning theories. In addition to cognitive tutors, other online instructional components include group experiments, virtual laboratories, and simulations. Courses include self-assessments and graded assessments (checkpoints and quizzes). There is also a Learn by Doing feature designed for students to better understand new concepts. The Learn by Doing activities include multiple choice, interactive simulations, and matching activities, to name a few. An example of an Osmosis Learning by Doing exercise in the Modern Biology course is provided in the OLI website.

In additional to the courses already mentioned, other open and free courses offered by Carnegie Mellon University (OLI) program are as follows:

- American English Speech

- Anatomy and Physiology

- Argument Diagramming

- Biochemistry

- Chemistry

- Elementary French I

- Elementary French II

- Engineering Statics

- Introduction to Biology

- Introduction to Chemistry

- Introduction to Psychology

- Media Programming

- Modern Biology

- Principles of Computing

- Probability of Statistics

- Responsible Computing

- Statistical Reasoning

- Stem Readiness

Carnegie Mellon University's OLI not only provides opportunities for students and educators, opportunities also abound for dedicated, forward-thinking individual collaborators, partner organizations, and strategic fundraisers to become involved and help the initiative grow and improve.

Yale University (Open Yale)

There are a variety of free university courses available online from distinguished universities such as Harvard, Carnegie Mellon, and Yale. These top universities offer free courses for a variety of reasons. Some offer free courses as a measurement tool for analyzing particular learning theories while others use the lectures to determine the popularity of distance learning. One commonality of university open courses is that they provide individuals with an opportunity to learn more.

Open Yale Courses provides a number of free courses. Although Open Yale does not offer certificates, credits, or degree options, Yale Summer Session offers a number of online courses with college credits. To learn more about that, visit **Yale Summer Session**.

Some of the courses offered at Open Yale are in:

- African American Studies

- Astronomy

- Biology

- Chemistry

- Economics

- English

- Environmental Studies

- Geology and Geophysics

- History

- Italian Language and Literature

- Political Science

- Psychology

- Religion

- Sociology

- Spanish and Portuguese

Participating in an Open Yale free course is simple. If you click on Introduction to Psychology (PSYC 110), for example, you are navigated to the course site, which provides a brief description of the course, instructor bio, and access to video and audio taken from course lectures via YouTube or iTunes. You also have the option to download all course materials in a zip file. The course sessions are composed of twenty lectures presented by assigned instructors and lecturers, a midterm, and a final exam.

Requirements for participating in the Introduction to Psychology course are to complete exams, complete reading assignments and responses, write a book review, and serve as a possible subject for class experiments.

Massachusetts Institute of Technology
MIT Opencourseware (OCW)

The popularity of free courses offered by top universities is growing, and one such university is MIT with its **Open Courseware (OCW)**. Composed of over 250 universities and organizations worldwide, MIT OCW Consortium is an independent nonprofit organization dedicated to sharing education worldwide by offering online publications of a wide variety of course content. Since its inception on April 4, 2001 when MIT announced it would publish all educational course materials openly on the Internet, OCW has shared materials from over 2,000 courses and reached an estimated 100 million people globally.

A free educational avenue such as this has the capacity to reach a variety of people, including educators seeking improved teaching methodologies, students seeking classes not available at their own universities, and independent learners finding ways to broaden their scope of learning. Using OCW's Course Finder can help interested parties locate courses by topic, sub-topic, and area of specialty. For instance, if one selects the topic of Teaching and Education, the sub-topics that display are as follows:

- Curriculum and Teaching

- Education Policy

- Education Measurement and Evaluation

- Education Technology

- Higher Education

- Instructional Media Design

- Professional Development

- Psychology and Research

Depending on the area of teaching and education in which you are interested, you can also filter the search results to the following delivery methods: video and audio lectures, student work, lecture notes, assessments, online textbooks, and interactive simulations. Furthermore, many of the courses have been translated to Traditional Chinese, Simplified Chinese, Spanish, Portuguese, Thai, Persian, Turkish, and Korean.

MIT OCW provides a global educational resource touching millions of people, and it would not have been possible without the help of hundreds of donors who have made this free educational system possible. The total annual cost to run MIT OCW is roughly $3.5 million, the money being spent to support faculty working to compile course materials and format for global distribution. Additionally, MIT OCW provides course content via rich media resources such as video lectures, animations, and simulations, all sustained through a complex technical infrastructure distributing courses worldwide.

Coursera

Coursera is an academic company that offers free education to individuals who are interested in learning. Coursera is partnered with various universities and organizations around the world to create a virtual classroom of international students. There are over 300 courses available that include computer science, mathematics, business, medicine, biology, social sciences, and humanities. Similar to some of the other open courseware classes available online, Coursera offers a free education with no college credit. The benefit is in the knowledge gained and shared during your educational journey.

To begin, you must first register with Coursera by providing your e-mail address and establishing a log-in password. Once your account has been created, you can browse the categories of courses and select your preferred language: English, Spanish, French, Chinese, German, or Italian. Since information technology is of interest to me, I selected the Building an Information Risk Management Toolkit offer from the University of Washington. The introductory page provides a short video narrated by the instructor, the date the class begins, the duration of the class, expected weekly hours of workload, and a Register button if you are interested. But be careful—once you hit that Register button, you are officially enrolled. If the timing of the class does not suit your schedule, you can add it to your watch list.

There is also an option called Signature Track that presents an opportunity to receive a Verified Certificate for completing a course at a specific university. For example, Jane Doe—Computer Science—Duke University, as well as a personal and secure URL to share your electronic course records with current or potential employers. Please review all terms of use associated with Signature Track courses because there may be fees for additional services provided. Courses are delivered via interactive quizzes, video lectures, peer-graded assessments, and web cam to interact with other students. Coursera also offers placement services for students seeking jobs within a specific field of study.

THE DECISION TO GO TO COLLEGE

The decision to go back to school can seem a bit daunting, particularly if you belong to Generation X-Y or are a baby boomer. But many people choose to go back to school for a variety of reasons: they may seek a change of career, have experienced job loss, need to improve their current job skills, hope to qualify for a promotion, or even seek personal enrichment. Once you have made the decision to return to school and are certain which degree you would like to pursue, the question remains: do you register for on-campus or distance learning? The method by which you have your education delivered is a very personal choice.

While distance learning sounds very convenient, you may benefit from the experiences that campus life offers. Perhaps you are an introvert yearning to step out of your shell, or perhaps you hope to acquire new friendships with other likeminded people. If this is the case, attending classes on campus is probably the best option for you initially. Attending brick-and-mortar classes can seem a bit intimidating at first, but stepping out of your comfort zone to experience real-life situations can provide you with a wealth of knowledge. You may learn lessons that allow you to blossom to your fullest potential. Not all lessons come from a college textbook; the social environment that college life offers can afford you with an opportunity to interact with a variety of students and to understand how to build relationships. Also, you never know who you might meet. Staying within your comfort zone does not nurture your potential for growth; instead, it diminishes the likelihood of your becoming the best person you can be. But, that doesn't mean there isn't a place for distance learning as well.

After experiencing college campus for a while, you may decide you're ready to divide your time between brick-and-mortar classes and distance learning classes. If you do not consider yourself to be a technologically savvy person, it would be wise to familiarize yourself with some tools mentioned in this book, they will provide the basic knowledge you need to ease into your distance learning experience.

Ultimately, your main goal is to learn. Whether you choose to study on campus or through distance learning, going back to school can be a life-changing experience that offers a wealth of knowledge, new skills, new friends, and a degree that can help you through your next chapter in life. The benefits are immeasurable. What are you waiting for?

Visit Distance Learning Books at
www.DistanceLearningBooks.Wordpress.com

THE AUTHOR

Patricia Pedraza-Nafziger is a Doctoral Candidate,
Contributing Editor for BellaOnline, and
Information Systems Team Lead for Boeing Company.
She enjoys spending time with her husband and two dogs,
traveling, cooking, outdoor recreation, and
considers herself a life-long-learner.

In her second book, *Distance Learning: Is it Right for You*,
Patricia shares lessons learned through her journey as a
distance learning student to help you decide
if distance learning is right
for you.

www.ingramcontent.com/pod-product-compliance
Lightning Source LLC
Chambersburg PA
CBHW061744020426
42331CB00006B/1347